Puzzle Quest

The lost emerald

Written & illustrated
by Kia Marie Hunt

Published by Collins
An imprint of HarperCollins Publishers
HarperCollins Publishers
Westerhill Road
Bishopbriggs
Glasgow G64 2QT

www.harpercollins.co.uk

HarperCollins Publishers
1st Floor, Watermarque Building
Ringsend Road
Dublin 4, Ireland

10 9 8 7 6 5 4 3 2

ISBN 978-0-00-853211-6

Printed and bound in the UK using 100% renewable electricity
at CPI Group (UK) Ltd

Publisher: Michelle I'Anson
Author and Illustrator: Kia Marie Hunt
Project Manager: Sarah Woods
Designer: Kevin Robbins

PUZZLE QUEST

The lost emerald

Written & illustrated
by Kia Marie Hunt

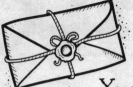

You've never received a letter like this before!

You unwrap the string and open the orange envelope's golden seal.

Inside is a letter from the residents of Cranksville, who tell you all about the leader of their kingdom:

King Cranky the Grumpy Goblin

This goblin already has a reputation for being rather prickly, but lately his mood has taken a turn for the worse after the emerald was stolen from his crown.

The creatures of Cranksville need you to investigate this crime and solve the mystery of Cranky's lost emerald!

Explore the castle and follow the evidence wherever it takes you. Be ready to solve more than 100 fun puzzles, investigating and collecting clues along the way!

Things you'll need:

- ★ **This book**
- ★ **A pen or pencil**
- ★ **Your amazing brain**

That's it!

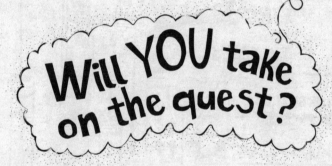

Psssst!
Always look out for
this paw symbol:

This means you've found a clue.

Write down all the clues you find in your Clue Logbooks
(on pages **30, 54, 78, 102** and **126!**)

CRANKY'S CASTLE

Soon, you'll be on your way to King Cranky's kingdom, Cranksville...

Be ready to take on a castle full of quests, majestic mind games and noble number fun.

Remember to look out for this paw symbol:

which means you've found a clue!
(Record all your clues in the logbook on Page 30.)

The royal crank-carriage is here to pick you up and take you all the way to King Cranky's castle.

Follow the numbers along each carriage from left to right and figure out which number is next in the sequence. Write the final numbers into the ovals.

13 27

6 20

8 24

16 32

36

31 26 21

The road to reach Cranky's Kingdom is very long and bumpy, but you don't mind – your journey in the crank-carriage is rather luxurious!

Follow the tangled paths. Which one will lead you all the way to King Cranky's Kingdom? Write your answer into this box.

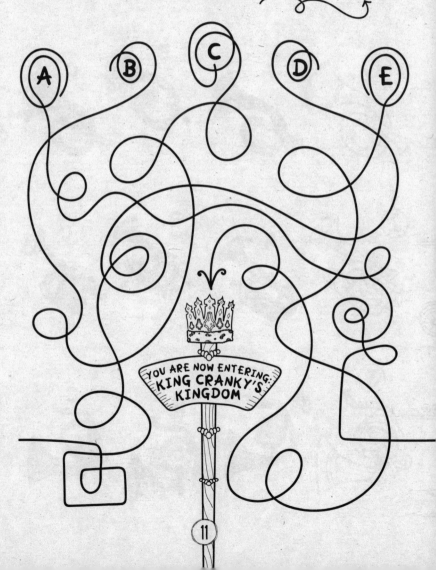

You must have fallen asleep somewhere along the way, because you suddenly wake up to the sound of trumpets and horns announcing your arrival.

Which silhouette correctly matches each instrument? Circle your answers.

Follow the lines and write the letter from each oval into the space at the end of each line to reveal a new word. The first letter of each word has already been done for you.

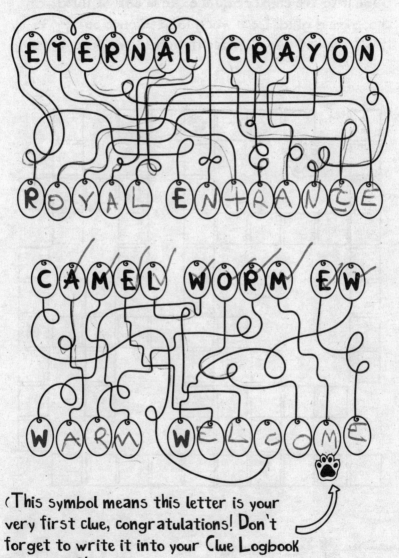

ETERNAL CRAYON

ROYAL ENTRANCE

CAMEL WORM EW

WARM WELCOME

(This symbol means this letter is your very first clue, congratulations! Don't forget to write it into your Clue Logbook on page 30!)

Wow, the castle is so ginormous that it makes the royal crank-carriage look tiny!

Place the castle words from the list on the opposite page into the empty squares to create a filled crossword grid. Each word is used once so cross it off the list as you place it to help you keep track.

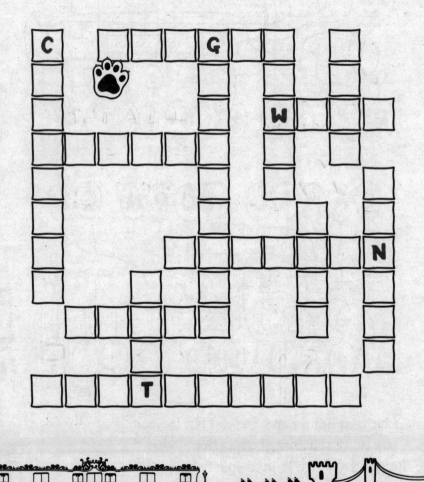

4 LETTERS
FORT
HALL
KEEP
WALL

5 LETTERS
STONE
TOWER

6 LETTERS
CANNON
KNIGHT
STABLE

7 LETTERS
DUNGEON

8 LETTERS
CROSSBOW

9 LETTERS
GATEHOUSE

10 LETTERS
BATTLEMENT

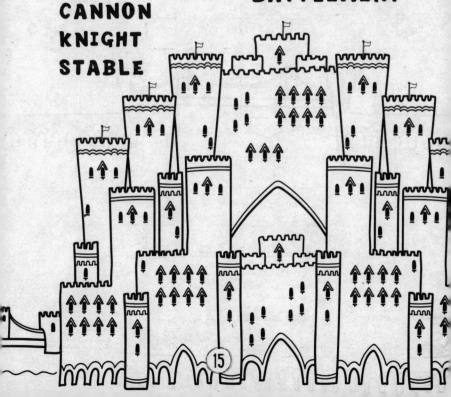

To cross the drawbridge and enter through the castle door, you must first say the secret password...

Scribble out every other letter from left to right across the bridge. Write the letters that are left over on the lines below to reveal the password. The first letter has already been done for you.

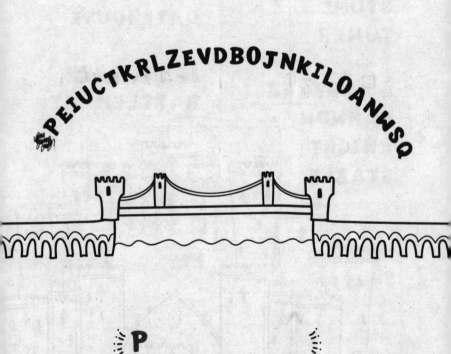

P _ _ _ _ _ _

_ _ _ _ _ _

The numbers 1, 2, 3 and 4 should be added to each row, each column and each 2x2 bold outlined box, but should only appear once in each one. The first one has been done for you.

As you step inside the huge castle doors, you find a small ghostly cat floating before you.

Use the symbol key to crack the code and fill in the gaps to reveal what the cat is saying to you.

A E I N O S U

"W_LC_M_ T_ K___ G CR__KY'

C_TL_! _'LL B_ Y__R G__D_.

F_LL_W M_ CL__LY B_C

TH_ _NCH__T_D C__TL_ P_TH_

M_V_ _R__ND _ L_T!"

Catsper, your castle guide, floats away down the corridors. While they glide through the air, you have to walk across the enchanted paths...

Be careful – the floating floor tiles can move around or disappear without warning!

Make your way from start to finish. You can move up, down or sideways, but you can't move diagonally and you must only follow the tiles with odd numbers. The line has been started off for you.

Catsper moves quickly, leading you along corridors, through candle-lit halls, into secret rooms behind bookcases, across bridges and even down some upside-down staircases!

Now you understand why you need a guide, it would be easy to get lost in this huge castle...

Can you make your way through the castle maze from start to finish?

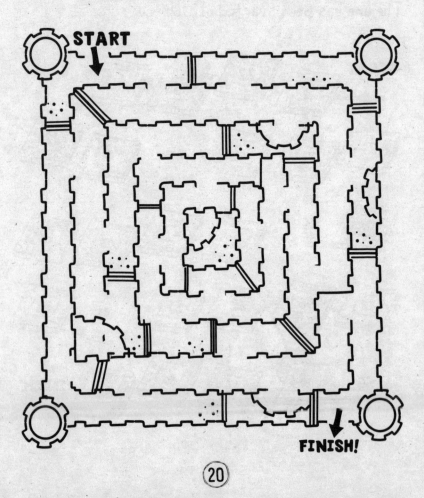

In the word-wheels, find three things you might see on the walls of an old castle. Each word starts with the centre letter and uses all the letters in the wheel once.

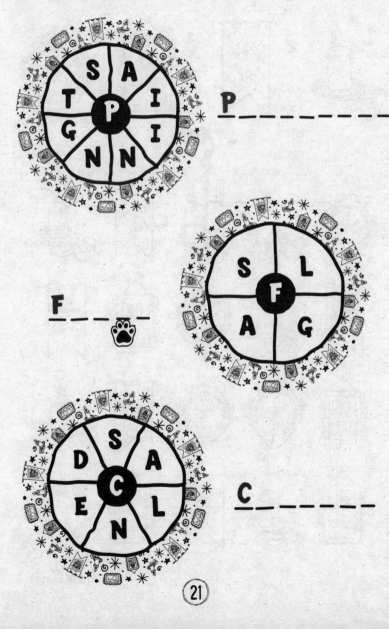

P _ _ _ _ _ _ _ _

F _ _ _ _ _

C _ _ _ _ _ _

Make your way from start to finish. You can move up, down or sideways but you can't move diagonally and you must follow the castle items in this order:

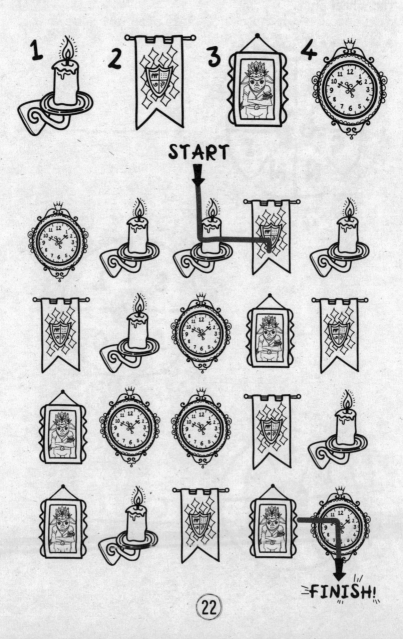

It's nearly time to meet King Cranky, who is waiting on the other side of the Royal Throne Room.

Odd one out: which royal throne does not have a matching pair? Circle your answer.

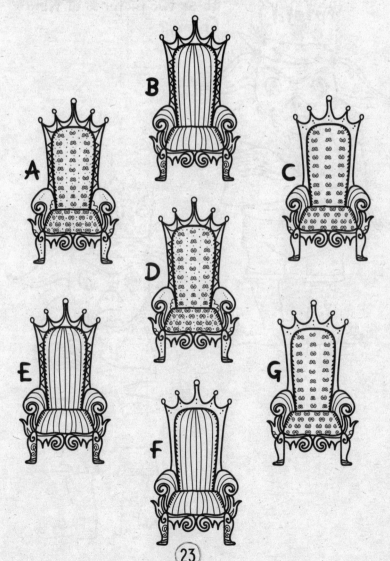

Everyone was right to warn you – King Cranky
really is the grumpiest goblin you have ever met!

Can you find and circle all
six differences between
these two pictures of King
Cranky?

Cranky isn't really interested in getting to know you. The only thing that's important to this goblin king is whether or not you can solve the mystery of the lost emerald!

Cross out any letter that appears more than once in the grid below. Write the letters that are left over on the lines below in the order they appear, and a hidden word will reveal itself. Letter K has been scribbled out to start you off.

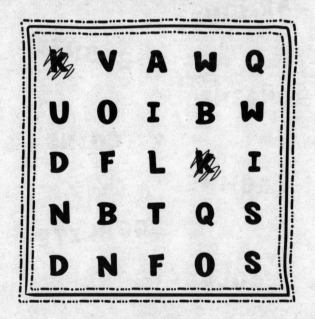

LET'S GO TO THE

_ _ _ _ _ !

Catsper unlocks the heavy gold door and leads you into the secure vault... or not-so-secure vault! This is where King Cranky's crown was locked up when someone, somehow, broke in and stole the large emerald from it.

ARMOUR

BRONZE

CHAINS

COINS

CROWN

GOBLETS

GOLD

SILVER

Can you find all eight treasure words from the list on the opposite page in the wordsearch below?

Words may be hidden horizontally or vertically.

```
            I U X
          V L S R R
        C O I N S A J
      B F S T S O C P S
    L T E V I C R O W N A
  F S I L V E R U P O V R C
B O E F T L L U A P K A M U S
T B N H T A H J W W P V K O R P S
C C M Y H E R M V S C L M G U D A G H
  A U E H I B R O N Z E R O R R S T
    T F G Q I S Q H G N H L O R E
      K X A A B Z R O T T D R T
        C H A I N S B N Y C L
          L S Z S A L P S M
            G E G Y E S E
              O V U T L
                S U S
```

Wait, what's that?

You find a suspicious object on the floor of the vault... could this be a clue that helps you solve the mystery of the lost emerald?

Complete the number problems below and write your answers in the boxes. Each item should have the same answer. The odd one out is the item you find in the vault. Which is it?

Ⓐ 26 + 28

=

Ⓑ 91 - 33

=

Ⓒ 6 x 9

=

Ⓓ 87 - 33

=

Catsper seems to know who that item belongs to!

Use the symbol key to crack the code and fill in the gaps to reveal what your ghostly cat friend tells you...

Symbol Key: A C E G I K L N O R S T V W

Decoded message:

THAT **COG** BELONGS TO ONE

OF THE **CLOCKWORKERS**!

LET'S GO AND **VISIT** THE

CLOCKWORK WING

OF THE **CASTLE** AND SEE

WHAT THEY HAVE TO DO

WITH ALL THIS...

CLUE LOGBOOK:
Cranky's Castle

Before you and Catsper continue with your investigation, take a minute to use this logbook to record any clues you have found so far in and around Cranky's Castle and the vault.

Remember, clues are pointed out by this symbol:

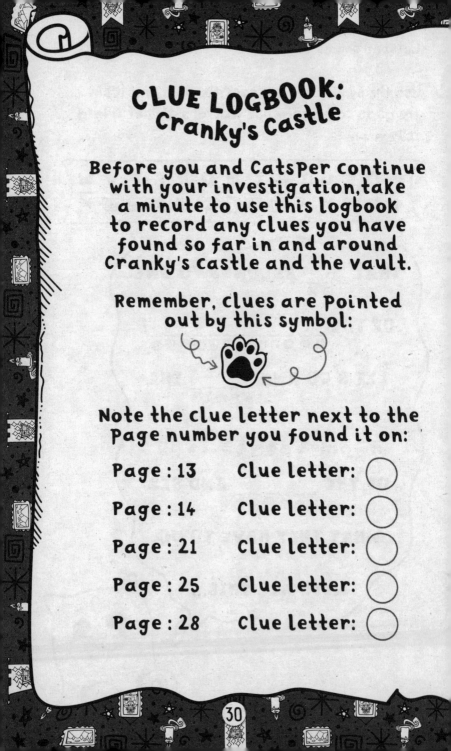

Note the clue letter next to the page number you found it on:

Page : 13   Clue letter: ◯

Page : 14   Clue letter: ◯

Page : 21   Clue letter: ◯

Page : 25   Clue letter: ◯

Page : 28   Clue letter: ◯

★ NOTES ★

M

(Blank 'notes' pages like this are handy
for jotting down any notes or working
out when you're busy solving puzzles!

You could also use them
to write, doodle or
anything else you'd
like to do while on
your quest!)

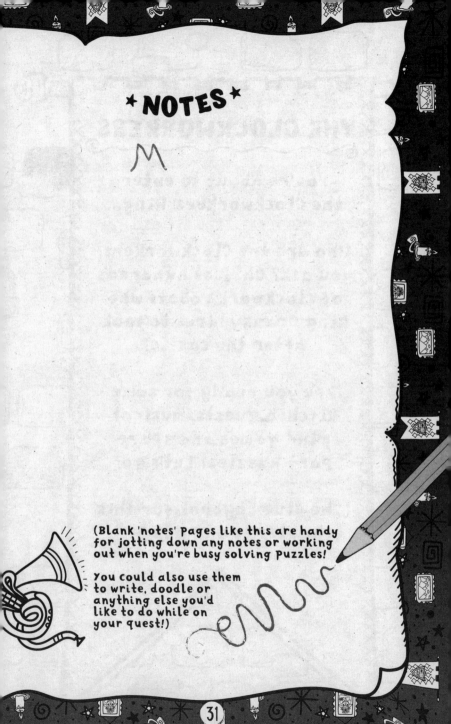

THE CLOCKWORKERS

You're about to enter
the Clockworkers' Wing...

Who are the Clockworkers,
you ask? Oh, just hundreds
of clockwork robots who
King Cranky hires to look
after the castle!

Are you ready for some
kitchen quests, musical
mind games and spare
part puzzles? Let's go!

(The Clue Logbook for this
chapter is on Page 54.)

It takes a lot of work to look after a whole castle, from cleaning all of the rooms and corridors, to feeding and entertaining King Cranky and his guests. Luckily, the Clockworkers love doing all kinds of jobs...

BAKER

BUTLER

CHEF

CLEANER

COOK

JESTER

KNIGHT

MUSICIAN

Can you find all eight of the job words from the list on the opposite page in the wordsearch below? Words may be hidden horizontally or vertically.

```
T R P Q U T S X S C M
B C L E P T F B P H S
E L P R U B B R Q E M
O E K N I G H T R F U
B A O V W S R U O W S
B N J S E D E C Z R I
A E X A R Q L K S H C
K R P O B U T L E R I
E J E S T E R F R O A
R C D T C O O K O R N
T U A J W F O S A R X
```

To begin your investigation, you start by
questioning all the cleaning Clockworkers,
who make sure the castle is kept spick and span.

Can you find all seven
differences between
these two cleaning
Clockworkers?

In the word-wheels, find three things these Clockworkers might use to clean the castle. Each word starts with the centre letter and uses all the letters in the wheel once.

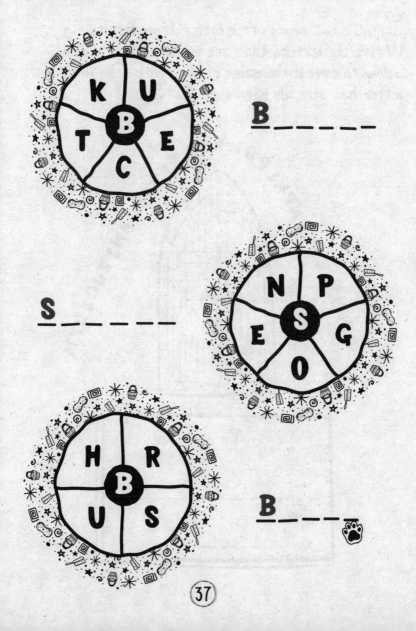

B _ _ _ _ _

S _ _ _ _ _

B _ _ _ _

You discover that the cleaning Clockworkers could not have stolen the lost emerald, as they were cleaning a very special room when it was taken.

Scribble out every other letter from left to right. Write the letters that are left over on the lines below to reveal the name of the room. The first letter has already been done for you.

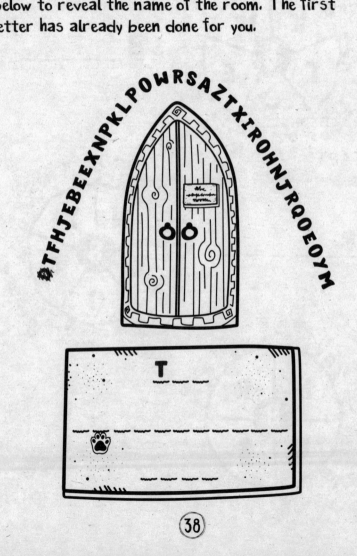

@TFHJEBEEXNPKLPOWRSAZTXIROHNJRQEOYM

T _ _

___ ___ ___ ___

___ ___ ___

This is where King Cranky keeps souvenirs from travels far and wide. The Clockworkers work hard to keep these precious items clean and dust-free!

Make your way from start to finish. You can move up, down or sideways but you can't move diagonally and you must follow the items in this order:

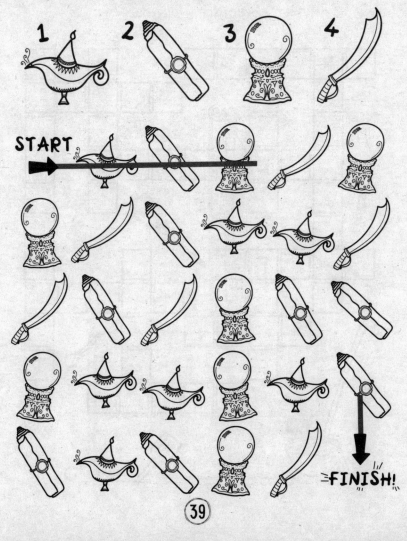

Next, you question the cooking Clockworkers. Where were all the cooks, chefs and bakers when the lost emerald was taken...?

Place the cooking words from the list on the opposite page into the empty squares to create a filled crossword grid. Each word is used once so cross it off the list as you place it to help you keep track.

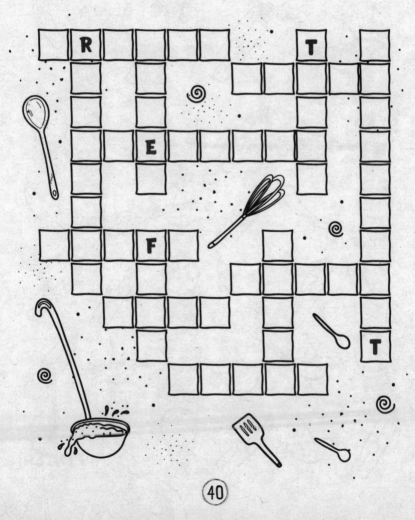

4 LETTERS

FORK

TRAY

5 LETTERS

GLASS

KNIFE

PLATE

SPOON

TIMER

TONGS

WHISK

6 LETTERS

GRATER

8 LETTERS

ROASTING

STEAMING

10 LETTERS

INGREDIENT

You discover that the cooking Clockworkers couldn't possibly have stolen the emerald, as they were all busy in the kitchens, preparing the royal banquet!

Follow the lines and write the letter from each oval into the space at the end of each line to reveal a new word. The first letter of each word has already been done for you.

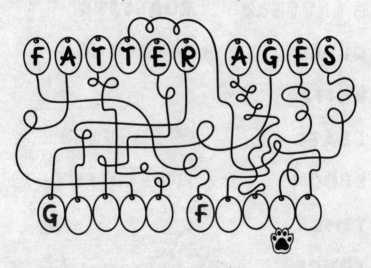

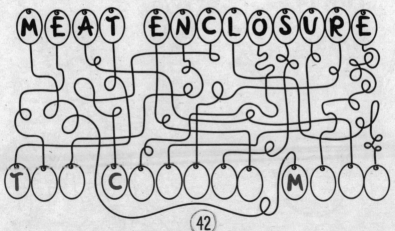

You stop for a moment to sample the delicious food and drink piled high on the banquet table. Investigating a missing jewel is hungry work!

Follow the numbers up each banquet tower and figure out which number is next in the sequence. Write the final numbers into the clouds at the top.

It's time to visit the entertaining Clockworkers:
the jokers, jesters, actors and musicians who
keep King Cranky and the royal guests amused.
You'll find them over in the castle theatre...

Can you make your way from the start, all the way
to the castle theatre at the centre of the maze?

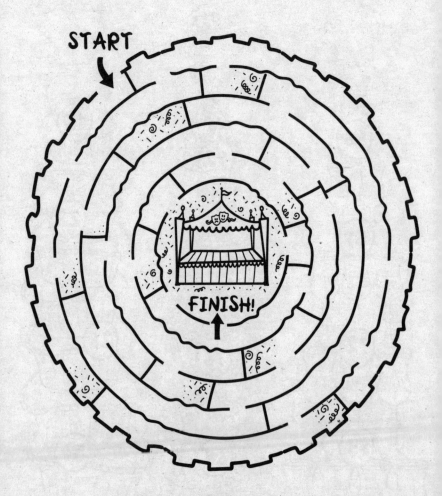

Odd one out: which musical Clockworker does not have an identical twin? Circle your answer.

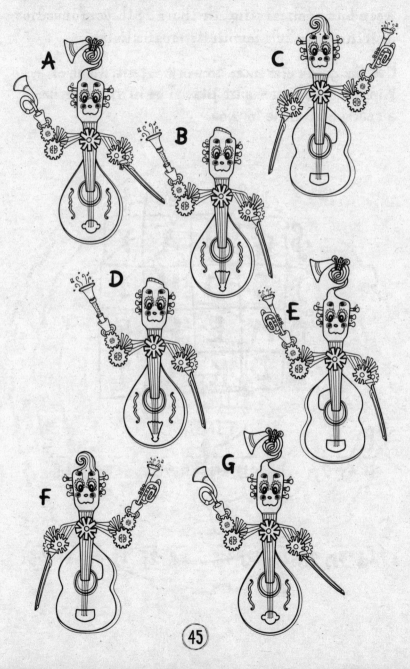

Yet again, you find your suspects are not guilty. While the emerald was taken, these Clockworkers were busy rehearsing for their 78th performance of King Cranky's favourite musical play.

Use the grid references to work out the name of King Cranky's favourite play. The first letter has already been done for you.

While you are here, you might as well stay for one performance. The jester Clockworkers are so funny, the actors in the play are so good and the songs are so catchy. You'll probably be humming their tunes for the rest of your quest!

Make your way from start to finish. You can move up, down or sideways but you can't move diagonally and you must only follow the theatre masks with even numbers. The line has been started off for you.

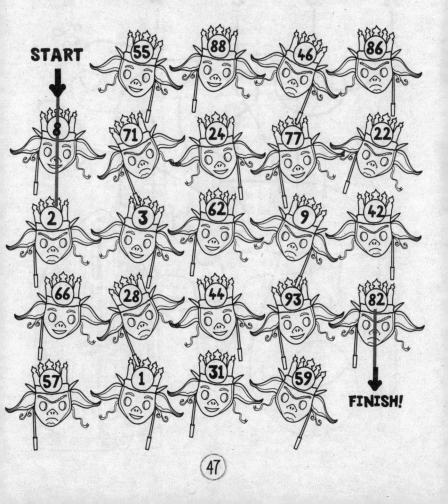

With no luck questioning your suspects so far, Catsper suggests going to investigate the Clockworkers' secret spare parts cupboard for any clues...

Follow the tangled paths. Which one leads to the secret spare parts cupboard?

To enter the secret spare parts cupboard, you and Catsper have to unscramble a set of cog passcodes.

The numbers 1, 2, 3 and 4 should be added to each row, each column and each 2x2 bold outlined box, but should only appear once in each one. The first one has been done for you.

3	2	1	4
4	1	2	3
1	3	4	2
2	4	3	1

			3
	3		
		1	
	2		

	4	1	
			4
3			
	1	3	

49

Inside, you find shelves stacked to the ceiling, full of cogs, wheels, pipes and other clockwork parts... but no emerald.

Which silhouette correctly matches each spare part? Circle your answers.

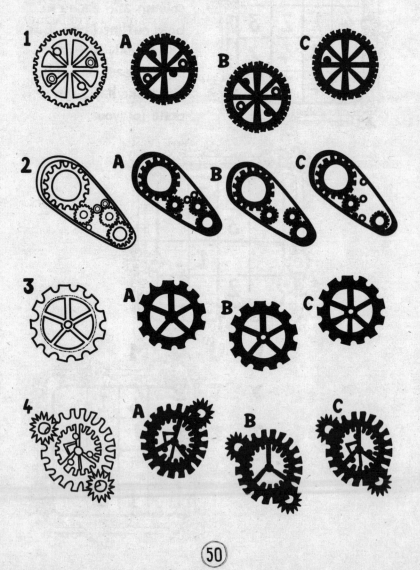

A tidying Clockworker is surprised to see you in their secret cupboard, but has an extra mission for you... the Clockworkers' back-up battery has gone missing!

Can you look out for it while you are investigating the case of the lost emerald? Solve the puzzle below to find out what the battery is made of...

Cross out any letter that appears more than once in the grid below. Write the letters that are left over on the lines below in the order they appear, and a hidden word will reveal itself. Letter D has been scribbled out to start you off.

A D L F H
K D F G N
L K U G M
N Y T B Y
H T E R U

___ ___ ___ ___ ___

So, now you are on the lookout for a lost emerald and a lost piece of amber. You have quite a lot to do!

What's that? You spot another potential clue on one of the cupboard shelves...

Complete the number problems below and write your answers in the boxes. Each item should have the same answer. The odd one out is the item you find on the shelf. Which is it?

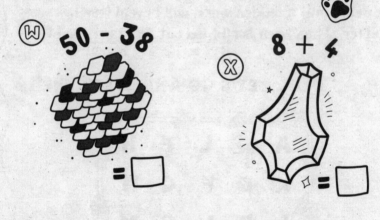

(W) 50 - 38 = ☐

(X) 8 + 4 = ☐

(Y) 3 x 4 = ☐

(Z) 40 - 27 = ☐

You ask Catsper for any ideas about where this clue might have come from.

Use the symbol Key to crack the code and fill in the gaps to reveal what your ghostly cat friend tells you...

A	E	F	G	H	I	L	N	P	R	S	T	U	V
✤	∷	◈	✕	★	👑	◎	▯	⊘	⛉	⚙	⊕	▣	✳

THAT F E A T H E R BELONGS TO
◈ ∷ ✤ ⊕ ★ ∷ ⛉

A G I A N _ M A G P I E !
✕ 👑 ✤ ▯ ⊕   ✤ ✕ ⊘ 👑 ∷

LET'S GO AND VISIT THE

_ _ _ _ _ _ _ _ _ _ UP IN
▯ ∷ ⚙ ⊕ ✳ ✕ ◎ ◎ ✤ ✕ ∷

THE CASTLE _ _ _ _ _ _ _
⊕ ▣ ⛉ ⊘ ∷ ⊕ ⚙

TO SEE WHAT WE

CAN FIND OUT...

53

CLUE LOGBOOK:
Clockworkers' Wing

Wow, it sure was fun to find out what all the castle's Clockworkers get up to, but you're still no closer to finding out what happened to the lost emerald...

Before you continue, make a note of any clues you found in this wing of the castle.

Note the clue letter next to the Page number you found it on:

Page : 37   Clue letter: ◯

Page : 38   Clue letter: ◯

Page : 42   Clue letter: ◯

Page : 46   Clue letter: ◯

Page : 51   Clue letter: ◯

Page : 52   Clue letter: ◯

★ NOTES ★

MAGPIE TURRETS

Next stop: the castle roof!

It's time for you and Catsper to visit the Nest Village, also known as 'Magpie Turrets'.

Smooth your feathers and prepare yourself for a whole rooftop full of turret tasks, nest number games and winged word fun.

(The Clue Logbook for this chapter is on page 78.)

To reach the Nest Village, you need to climb to the top of the castle's tallest turrets!

The numbers 1, 2, 3 and 4 should be added to each row, each column and each 2x2 bold outlined box, but should only appear once in each one. The first one has been done for you.

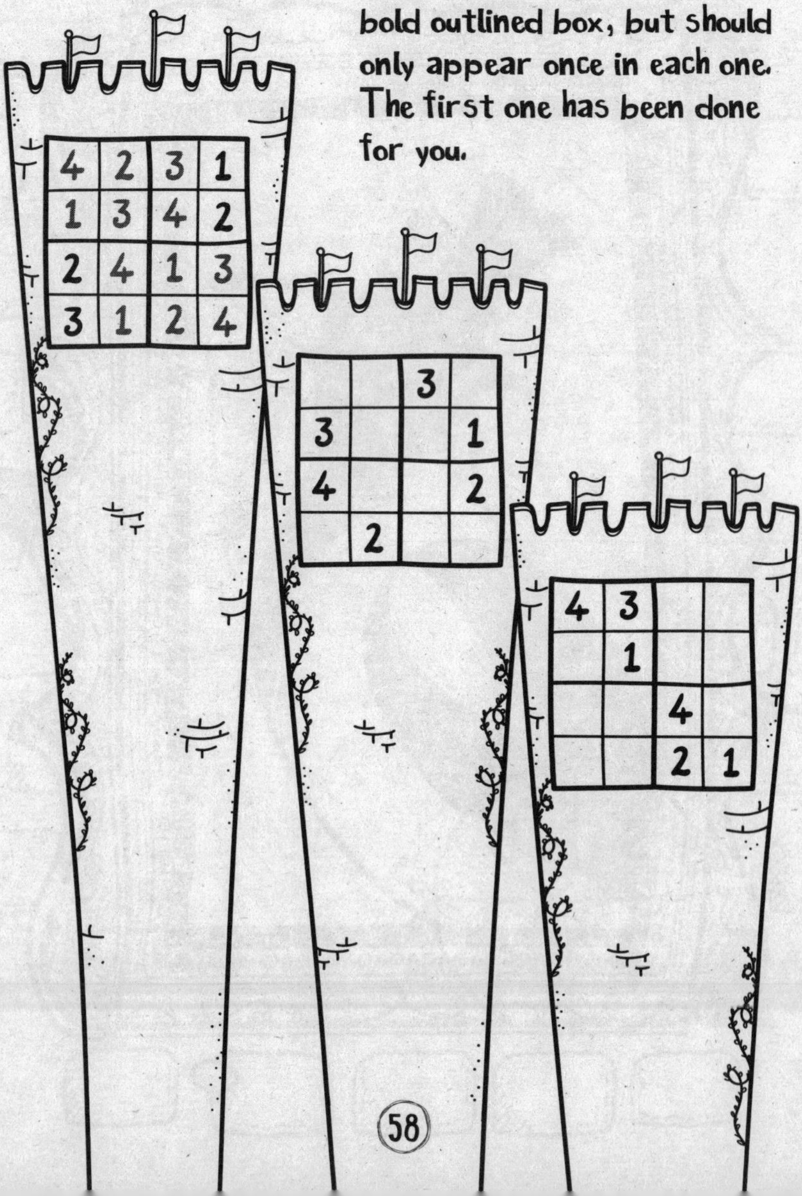

Puzzle 1 (completed):

4	2	3	1
1	3	4	2
2	4	1	3
3	1	2	4

Puzzle 2:

		3	
3			1
4			2
	2		

Puzzle 3:

4	3		
	1		
			4
		2	1

In the word-wheels, find three things you could climb up to reach a higher place. Each word starts with the centre letter and uses all the letters in the wheel once.

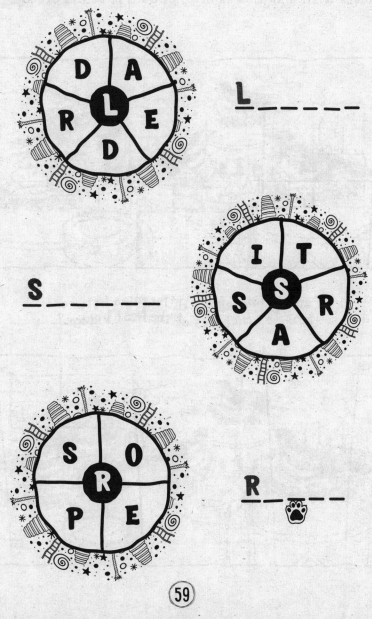

L _ _ _ _ _

S _ _ _ _ _ _

R _ _ _ _

Up on the roof of the castle, you enter what feels like a whole new world. Here, amongst the tops of the turrets, there is a whole village of giant birds' nests with magpies as big as buses perched on top!

Can you find all six differences between these two pictures of the Nest Village?

Cranksville is home to a few species of giant bugs. As King Cranky is so afraid of insects, the birds are allowed to live here if they agree to eat any bug they see within three miles of the castle!

The birds love to live up high. What's more, all those nests act like a thatched roof that keeps Cranky's castle nice and warm.

```
P E A A P E M A G M
M G M E I P I M I A
I P M E I A A E M G
G I M E A P G A A A
M G P A G I I P G I
M G P G G A A M P M
E A P A I A I M I A
M P E G A G G M E G
I G M G M A G M G E
M G I P M G P E I I
```

The word 'MAGPIE' has been hidden in the grid above. Can you find the complete word? The word may be hidden horizontally or vertically.

The local residents of Cranky's Kingdom have nicknamed the Nest Village 'Magpie Turrets' after all the giant magpies who live here. But many don't realise that lots of other kinds of birds live up here too!

3 LETTERS
JAY
OWL

6 LETTERS
THRUSH

7 LETTERS
SPARROW

4 LETTERS
CROW
WREN

8 LETTERS
PHEASANT
STARLING

5 LETTERS
RAVEN
ROBIN

9 LETTERS
BLACKBIRD
PARTRIDGE

Place the bird words from the list on the opposite page into the empty squares below to create a filled crossword grid. Each word is used once so cross it off the list as you place it to help you keep track.

There are a lot of nests in the Nest Village, but that's not all – there is a whole bird world up here!

Solve the number problem below each letter in the Key. Then use the answers to fill in the gaps and reveal some of the names on the signpost. One letter has been done for you.

Key

A	C	E	H	L	M	N
10−8	8−4	3×4	30÷5	4+9	5×3	27÷9
2						

O	R	S	T	U	W	Y
24÷3	40÷8	14−7	4×4	27÷3	8+6	19−8

FOUR F _A_ _ _ _ _ CAFE
       12 2 16 6 12 5 7

_A_ _ _ _ BIRDS   _ _ _ _ _ _
12 2 5 13 11   3 9 5 7 12 5 11

_ _ _ _ _ 'N' STUFF
14 8 5 15 7

B_ _ _ _ _ _ _ BUYS
 12 7 16 3 12 7 16

BACK TO _A_ _ _ _ _
        4 2 7 16 13 12

_ _ _ BIRD BA_ _ _ _
16 6 12   2 16 6 7

Uh oh! Even as a ghost, Catsper is still a cat who loves to chase birds. Off at top speed, Catsper floats away to chase a giant fluffy chick. Quick, catch up!

Follow the tangled paths. Which one leads you all the way to Catsper?

Catsper isn't the only one who is easily distracted... You forget about your investigation for a while as you explore the Nest Village and learn a new skill!

Scribble out every other letter from left to right. Write the letters that are left over on the lines below to reveal the name of the workshop you try out. The first five letters have already been done for you.

STOHRETOFRHANCXLAESORWTLWSFNMEZSQTRB
YUJILLPDDIFNJGBMRAFSJTKEIRACBLQARSTS

THE OR___ ___'_

___ __-_____

_____

Each learner in the class is given some nesting materials to build with: sticks, moss balls, leafy branches and twigs.

Make your way from start to finish. You can move up, down or sideways but you can't move diagonally and you must follow the nesting materials in this order:

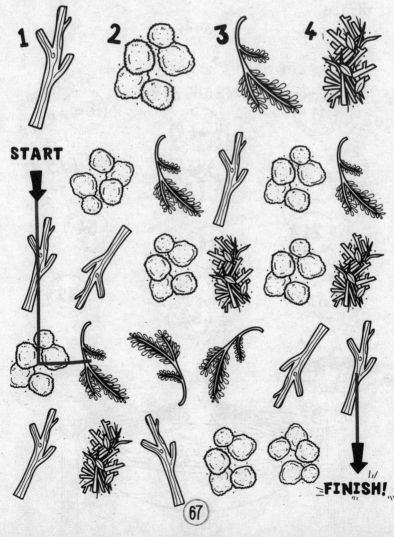

START

FINISH!

After building a cosy nest, you continue exploring. Next stop, the Bird Baths, where feathered friends go for a soak to rest their weary wings.

Follow the numbers up each stream of bubbles and figure out which number is next in the sequence. Write the final numbers into the popped bubbles at the top.

The Bird Baths are built on top of the castle kitchens, where the heat rising from chimneys keeps the bath water warm and bubbling.

Follow the lines and write the letter from each bubble into the space at the end of each line to reveal new words. Some letters have already been done for you.

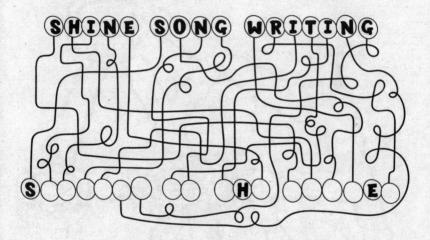

After a few fun distractions, you and Catsper decide to get back to the investigation. It's time to question the residents of the Nest Village.

Travel the paths to visit each nest once.
Only use one straight line to connect each nest and whatever you do, don't travel along the same path twice!

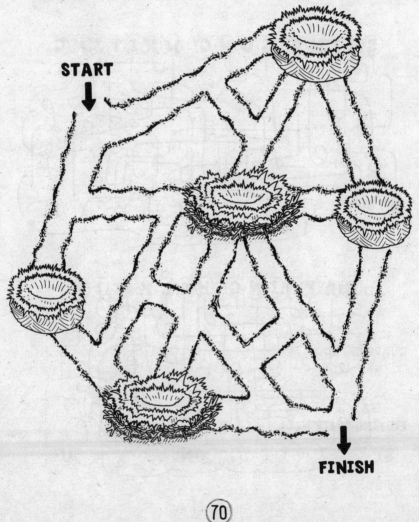

START

FINISH

After a long walk around, you figure out that none of the birds could've taken the emerald, as they were all doing something else at the time!

Match each pair of number problems to the correct answer to find out which bird was doing each activity. The first one has been done for you.

4 x 14
TAKING A BATH ←
30 + 26

36 ÷ 2
HUNTING INSECTS
6 x 3

5 x 13
GATHERING TWIGS
43 + 22

50 - 17
COLLECTING SHINY THINGS
11 x 3

9 x 9
GUARDING EGGS
62 + 19

63 ÷ 3
TIDYING THEIR NEST
3 x 7

None of the birds you question could have taken the emerald, but just in case, Catsper takes you to investigate the Magpies' secret treasure stash – a huge nest where they hide all of their favourite shiny objects and treasures...

BEADS

BEETLES

BRACELETS

BUTTONS

FOIL

KEYS

NECKLACES

WATCHES

Can you find all eight of the shiny objects from the list on the opposite page in the wordsearch below?

Words may be hidden horizontally or vertically.

```
T O B B E E T L E S B
E W S S B E A D S N Y
T A X S B N X L O E M
U T T Q R D S I O C A
Y C R N A S L D E K L
T H C R C U D U E L A
W E J A E F O I L A M
E S U O L N Q G T C K
A X R X E C L M Q E E
H V B U T T O N S S Y
L Z I R S G P V D S S
C G L R L R L G R N A
```

Odd one out: which of the Magpies' special buttons does not have an identical twin? Circle your answer.

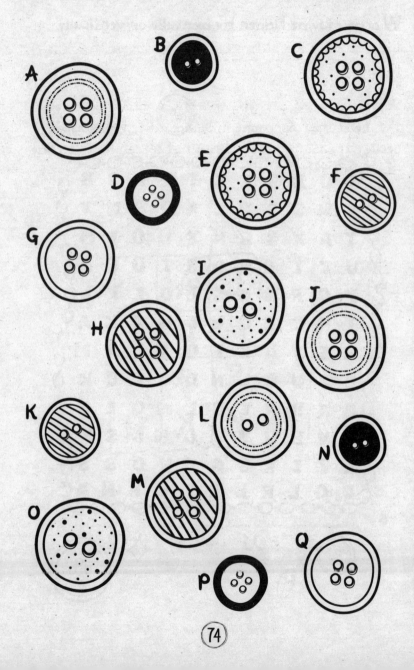

You don't find an emerald hidden anywhere, but you do find an angry magpie!

They make you a deal: they won't throw you into bird jail for breaking into their secret stash, as long as you help them find their stolen jewel too...

Use the grid references to work out the name of the jewel that has gone missing from the Magpies' secret treasure stash. The first letter has already been done for you.

S _ _ _ _ _ _ _ _
2◇ 3✦ 1⊛ 1⊛ 4🐞 4⊛ 1🐞 2✦

Yet again, instead of finding answers, all you have found is more questions! You now have not one but three missing gems to find... but you do find another clue in the Magpies' secret treasure stash.

Complete the number problems below and write your answers in the boxes. Each item should have the same answer. The odd one out is the item you find in the stash. Which is it?

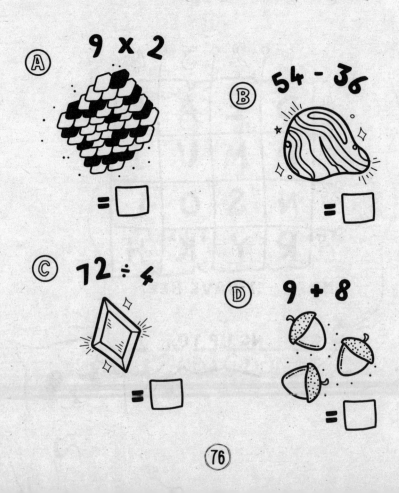

(A) 9 × 2 =

(B) 54 − 36 =

(C) 12 ÷ 4 =

(D) 9 + 8 =

Another clue! Where could this lead you and Catsper this time?

Use the symbol key to crack the code and fill in the gaps to reveal what your ghostly cat friend tells you...

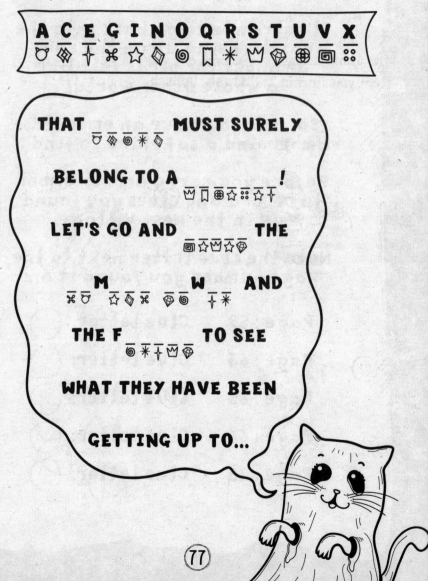

Symbol Key: A C E G I N O Q R S T U V X

THAT _ _ _ _ _ MUST SURELY

BELONG TO A _ _ _ _ _ _ _ !

LET'S GO AND _ _ _ _ _ THE

_ _ M _ _ _ _ W _ _ AND

THE F _ _ _ _ _ TO SEE

WHAT THEY HAVE BEEN

GETTING UP TO...

CLUE LOGBOOK: Magpie Turrets

It's strange to go back into the castle; being up on the roof amongst the birds felt like a whole other world!

So, now you have an emerald, amber and a sapphire to find...

Before you carry on, remember to record any clues you found up in the Nest Village.

Note the clue letter next to the page number you found it on:

Page : 59   Clue letter: ◯

Page : 63   Clue letter: ◯

Page : 65   Clue letter: ◯

Page : 66   Clue letter: ◯

Page : 75   Clue letter: ◯

★ NOTES ★

SQUIXIE FOREST

Cranksville is home to many weird and wonderful creatures, including a large population of squirrel-pixies known as 'Squixies'!

Are you ready to meet the Squixies and take on some quizzical card games, nature number fun and woodland word puzzles? Let's leap into it!

(The Clue Logbook for this chapter is on Page 102.)

There are probably some Squixies in the Gaming Tower with King Cranky right now, so you and Catsper set off to find them...

Can you get there by making your way through the maze from start to finish, adding up the points as you go over them? Watch out, you must only collect a total of 25 points on the way — any more or any less means you have gone the wrong way!

START

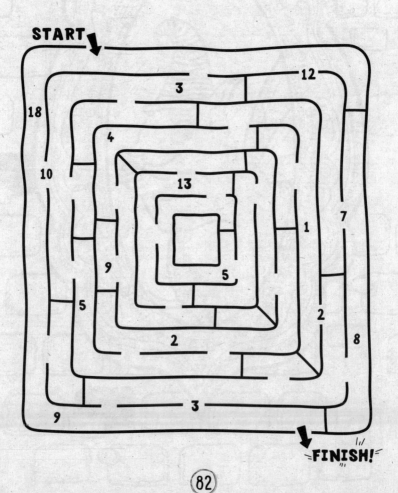

12

3

18

4

10

13

1

7

9

5

5

2

8

2

3

9

FINISH!

This tower is where King Cranky and his friends spend time playing board games and card games. There are solid gold and silver dice all over the place!

Make your way from start to finish. You can move up, down or sideways but you can't move diagonally and you must only follow the dice with an odd number of dots.

START

FINISH!

As expected, you find King Cranky in the Gaming Tower with three Squixies. Meeting them, you can now understand how these squirrel-pixie creatures got their name.

Use the grid references to work out the names of the three Squixies. The first letter has already been done for you.

You continue with your investigation by asking each Squixie what they were doing when the crime took place...

Which silhouette correctly matches each Squixie? Circle your answers.

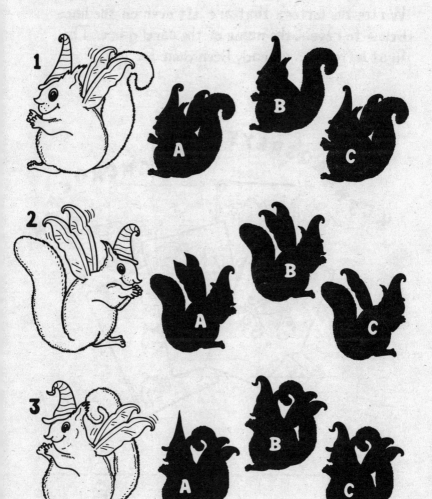

When the emerald was stolen from the vault, these Squixies were playing their favourite card game here in the Gaming Tower, just like they are right now with King Cranky!

Scribble out every other letter from left to right. Write the letters that are left over on the lines below to reveal the name of the card game. The first letter has already been done for you.

C _ _ _ _   _ _ _   _ _ _ _ _

You can join in with a game if you like, but you have to let King Cranky win or you'll be kicked out of the castle... that's not fair, what a grump!

Make your way from start to finish. You can move up, down or sideways but you can't move diagonally and you must follow the playing cards in this order:

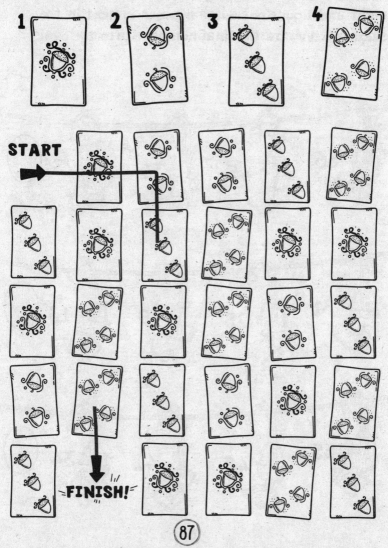

1   2   3   4

START

FINISH!

The Squixies in the Gaming Tower aren't guilty, so it's time to question the forest Squixies who live just beyond the castle walls. The easiest (and most fun) way to get there is to take the chairlifts from the towers to the trees!

Follow the numbers along each chairlift from left to right and figure out which number is next in the sequence. Write the final numbers into the ovals.

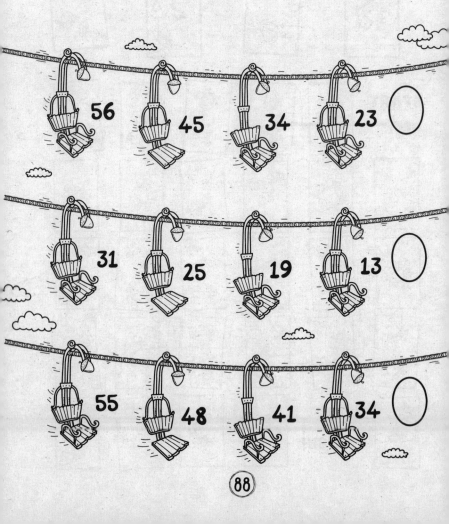

56   45   34   23   ( )

31   25   19   13   ( )

55   48   41   34   ( )

Hold on tight, the little wooden chairs whizz through the air at quite a speed! Don't look down...

Follow the lines and write the letter from each cloud into the space at the end of each line to reveal a new word. The first letter of each word has already been done for you.

The Squixies share their forest with many other woodland creatures. You spot plenty of wildlife scurrying around down below while you glide through the trees on your chair and Catsper floats along beside you.

3 letters
BAT
FOX
OWL

4 letters
DEER
FROG
NEWT
TOAD
VOLE

5 letters
OTTER
STOAT

6 letters
WEASEL

7 letters
BUZZARD

8 letters
DORMOUSE
SQUIRREL

9 letters
BUTTERFLY

Place the woodland creature words from the list on the opposite page into the empty squares below to create a filled crossword grid. Each word is used once so cross it off the list as you place it to help you keep track.

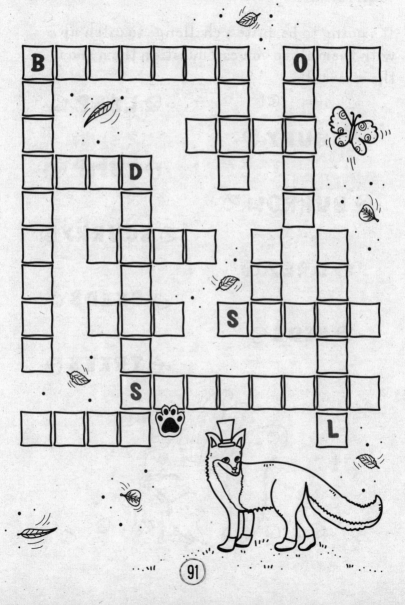

Finally, you reach the part of the forest where the Squixies live. Even though these squirrel-pixie creatures can fly, they still enjoy running and leaping through the trees just like all squirrels do!

It's going to be quite a challenge to catch up with them all so you can question them about the emerald...

·🌰 **LEAP** 🌰·

·🌰 **BURY** 🌰·

·🌰 **JUMP** 🌰·

·🌰 **BURROW** 🌰·

·🌰 **SCURRY** 🌰·

·🌰 **DREY** 🌰·

·🌰 **SEEDS** 🌰·

·🌰 **HIDE** 🌰·

·🌰 **TREES** 🌰·

Watch out! A word is missing...

Can you find eight of the nine squirrel words from the list on the opposite page hidden in the wordsearch below? Words may be hidden horizontally or vertically.

L	E	A	P	A	B	S	R	U	U	D
T	W	T	I	X	B	U	R	R	O	W
R	S	P	P	S	N	P	L	X	C	U
E	V	T	F	E	T	S	O	C	J	O
E	R	G	Z	E	Y	T	B	R	Z	U
S	S	I	S	D	R	O	P	S	Z	B
K	E	B	L	S	C	U	R	R	Y	U
Y	J	C	L	I	Q	D	R	E	Y	R
J	J	U	M	P	W	A	U	G	T	Y

Which word is missing from the wordsearch?

_ _ _ _ _ _ _

Some of the Squixies are talented royal carpenters who were busy carving wooden furniture for the castle when the emerald was taken.

Odd one out: which of these royal cabinets does not have a matching pair? Circle your answer.

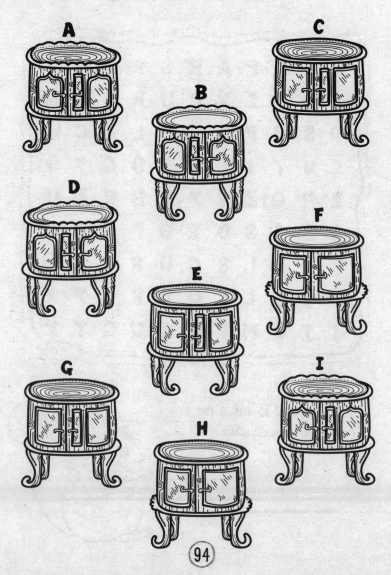

Other Squixies were out gathering ingredients from the forest to take to the castle kitchens for the cooking Clockworkers to use.

Can you unscramble the letters to reveal five different ingredients you might find in a forest? The first letter of each word has been done for you.

SERERIB → B _ _ _ _ _ _

SOMMRUSHO → M _ _ _ _ _ _ _

STUN → N _ _ _

TRUFI → F _ _ _ _

DESSE → S _ _ _ _

Some of the Squixies were busy taking some of the gathered ingredients to special hiding places, preparing the stores for the coming winter.

Match each pair of number problems to the correct answer to find out which food was stored in each hiding place. The first one has been done for you.

38 ÷ 2
IN THE CASTLE TUNNELS
40 − 21

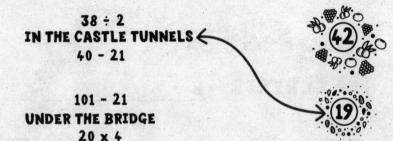

101 − 21
UNDER THE BRIDGE
20 x 4

6 x 7
IN THE MOSS CAVES
14 x 3

100 − 36
IN THE BADGER'S BURROW
8 x 8

13 x 2
UNDER THE OAK TREE
17 + 9

16 ÷ 4
IN THE SECRET DEN
22 − 18

Catsper has an idea: why don't you search the Squixies' secret den for the emerald or any clues? You can get there on the forest train!

Follow the tangled train tracks. Which one leads to the door of the secret storage den?

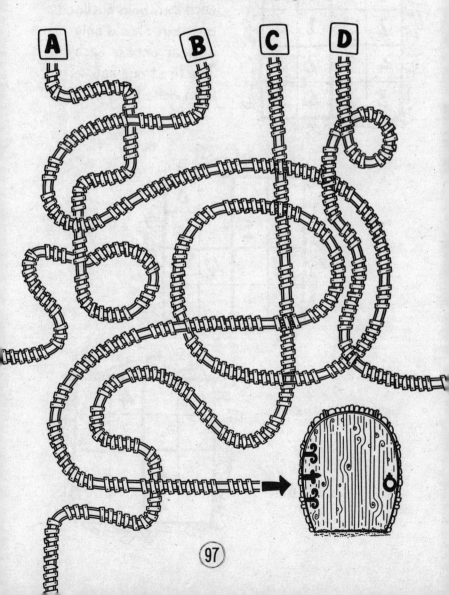

To enter the Squixies' secret storage den, you and Catsper have to unscramble a set of passcodes.

The numbers 1, 2, 3 and 4 should be added to each row, each column and each 2x2 bold outlined box, but should only appear once in each one. The first one has been done for you.

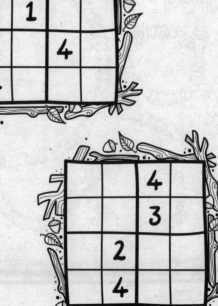

Wow, there are thousands of nuts stored in here!

In the word-wheels, find three nuts. Each word starts with the centre letter and uses all the letters in the wheel once.

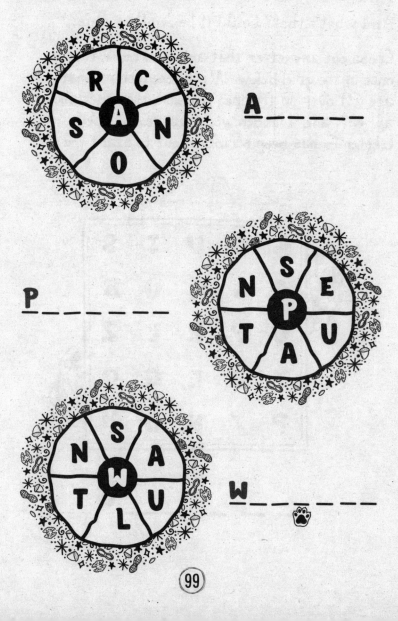

A _ _ _ _ _ _

P _ _ _ _ _ _

W _ _ _ _ _ _

Do you find anything else in the secret den? Only another mystery! A Squixie there tells you about their precious piece of yellow citrine that has gone missing...

And what's that? Could it be another clue?

Cross out any letter that appears more than once in the grid below. Write the letters that are left over on the lines below in the order they appear, and a hidden word will reveal itself. Letter G has been scribbled out to start you off.

G O U I S
C I A O B
U P Z L Z
Y B E G Q
P Y H Q H

___ ___ ___ ___ ___ S

Catsper usually seems so confident, but now your ghostly cat friend looks quite scared!

Use the symbol key to crack the code and fill in the gaps to reveal what your ghostly cat friend tells you...

A	C	D	E	G	H	I	L	N	O	R	S	T	U

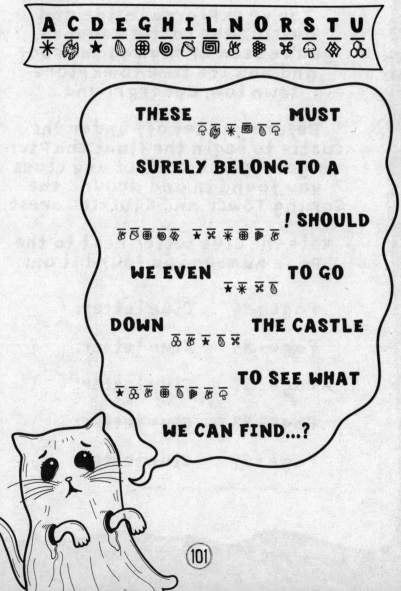

THESE _____ MUST

SURELY BELONG TO A

_____! SHOULD

WE EVEN _____ TO GO

DOWN _____ THE CASTLE

_____ TO SEE WHAT

WE CAN FIND...?

CLUE LOGBOOK: Squixie Forest

You've explored inside and outside the castle grounds, you've been up high to the roof and now it's time to explore down low, underground...

Before you set off under the castle to begin the final chapter of your quest, collect any clues you found in and around the Gaming Tower and Squixie Forest.

Note the clue letter next to the page number you found it on:

Page : 84   Clue letter: ◯

Page : 86   Clue letter: ◯

Page : 91   Clue letter: ◯

Page : 95   Clue letter: ◯

Page : 99   Clue letter: ◯

★NOTES★

DRAGON'S LAIR

Are you brave enough to
venture deep down under
the castle, all the way into
the Night Dragon's lair?

If you are, prepare
yourself for all kinds
of cave quests,
treasure tasks and
magical mysteries.

What will you discover in
this last part of your
adventure...?

(The Clue Logbook for this
chapter is on Page 126.)

You follow Catsper under the castle, who turns every so often to check again, "Are you sure!?"

Yes, you're sure. Together you continue into the darkness, going below the basement, then below the secret tunnels, and even below the dungeons!

Can you make your way down through the maze from start to finish?

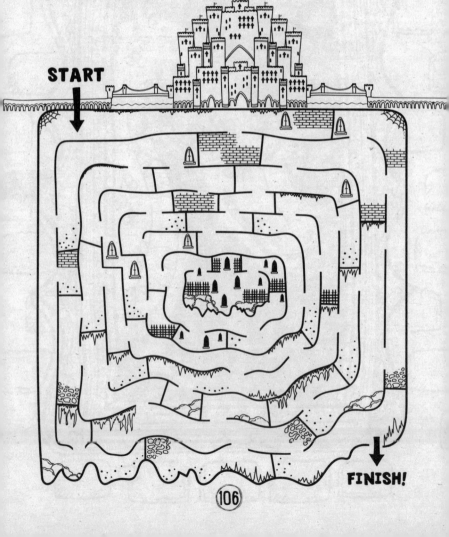

START

FINISH!

In the word-wheels, find three things you could use to light up the dark passageways. Each word starts with the centre letter and uses all the letters in the wheel once.

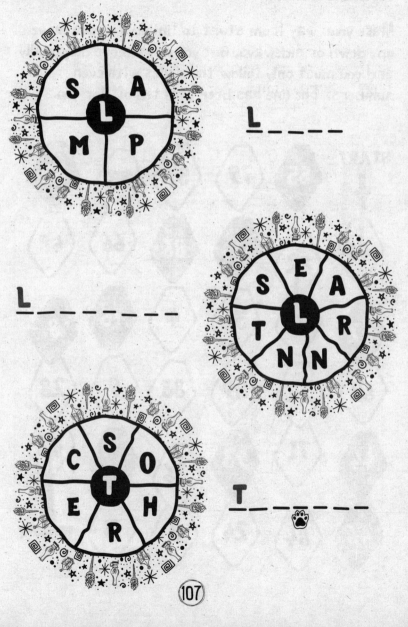

L _ _ _ _

L _ _ _ _ _ _ _

T _ _ _ _ _

Every so often, you find a shedded dragon scale or two on the floor, just like the ones you found in the Squixies' secret den. You must be going in the right direction...

Make your way from start to finish. You can move up, down or sideways, but you can't move diagonally and you must only follow the scales with even numbers. The line has been started off for you.

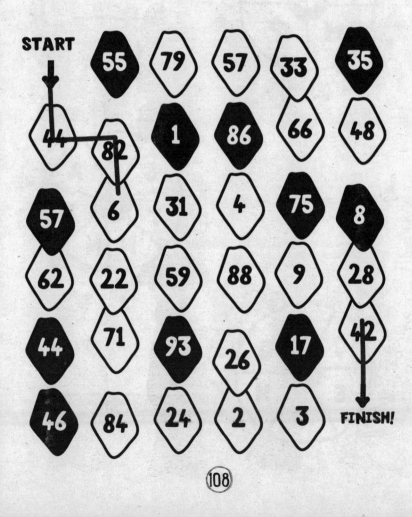

It's scary down here. The darkness plays tricks on you, making you think you're surrounded by creatures. To your relief, they are just strange rock towers and cave formations casting shadows!

Which silhouette correctly matches each formation? Circle your answers.

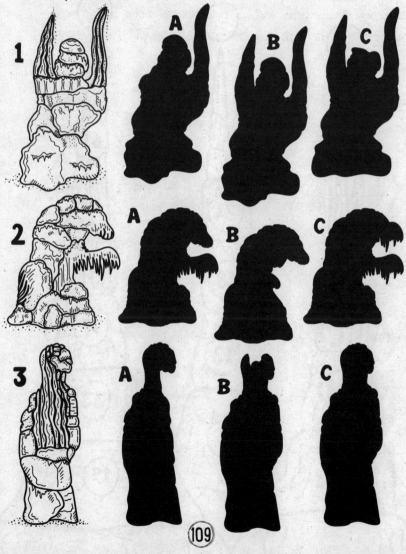

The deeper you go down underground, the taller the cave towers become!

Follow the numbers up each stalagmite tower and figure out which number is next in the sequence. Write the final numbers into the circles at the top.

Eventually, you reach a wide chamber with many different dark cave entrances. Which one will Catsper lead you into?

Complete the number problems below and write your answers in the boxes. Each cave should have the same answer. The odd one out is the cave you enter. Which is it? Write your answer in the box.

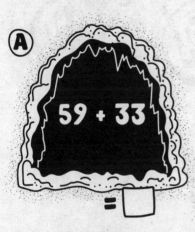

A 59 + 33 =

B 123 - 33 =

C 180 ÷ 2 =

D 9 x 10 =

You step inside the cave and you can't believe your eyes. This must be the Night Dragon's lair because there is a whole hoard of treasures to explore here!

Odd one out: which treasure does not have a matching pair? Circle your answer.

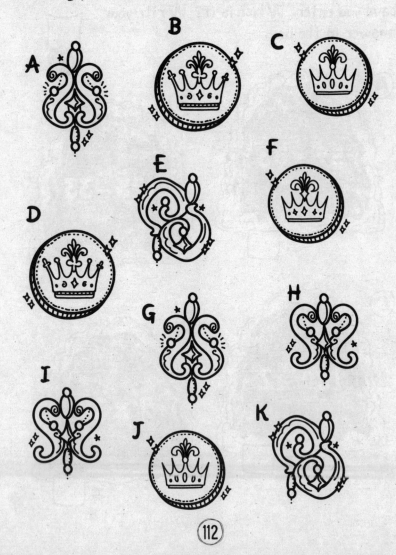

There are many of the precious treasures you would expect to see in a dragon's hoard, like encrusted swords, jewellery and coins. But it looks like the dragon also likes to collect some very unusual 'treasures' too!

Make your way from start to finish. You can move up, down or sideways but you can't move diagonally and you must follow the strange 'treasures' in this order:

You hunt through the treasures in the dragon's hoard to try to find King Cranky's emerald, the Clockworkers' amber, the Magpies' sapphire or the Squixies' citrine...

The numbers 1, 2, 3 and 4 should be added to each row, each column and each 2x2 bold outlined box, but should only appear once in each one. The first one has been done for you.

3	1	2	4
4	2	3	1
2	4	1	3
1	3	4	2

4		2	
	3		4

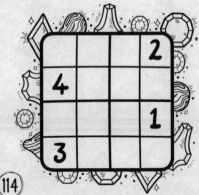

			2
4			
			1
3			

None of the lost or stolen jewels you're trying to find are here! Hmm, how strange, you were sure you had finally solved the mystery...

Wait, what was that? Can you hear something echoing down through one of the cave tunnels?

Use the grid references to work out each letter and reveal three words. The first letter has already been done for you.

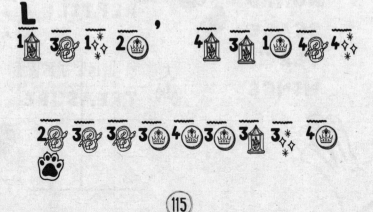

Uh oh! It sounds like the Night Dragon is coming closer. Catsper is nervous and wants to leave, but you are feeling brave...

How will you solve this mystery if you don't have the courage to stand tall and talk to the dragon?

4 LETTERS
CAVE
GOLD
HORN
LAIR
TAIL

6 LETTERS
SILVER

5 LETTERS
CLAWS
GREEN
HOARD
SCALE
TEETH
WINGS

7 LETTERS
MAGICAL
REPTILE

8 LETTERS
TREASURE

Place the dragon words from the list on the opposite page into the empty squares below to create a filled crossword grid. Each word is used once so cross it off the list as you place it to help you keep track.

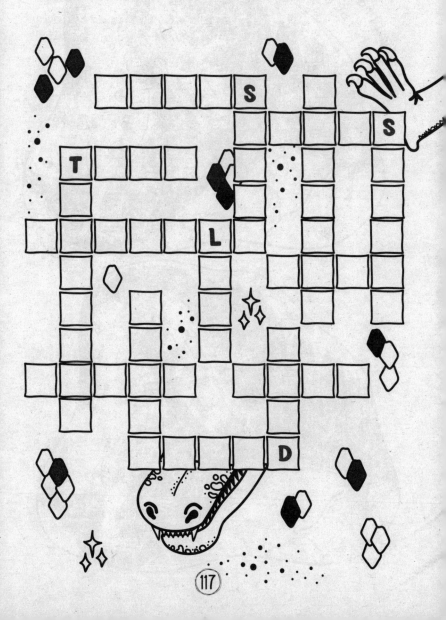

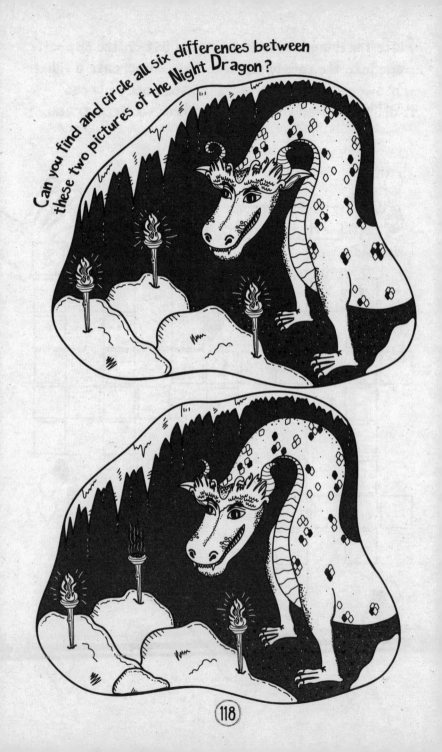

At first, the enormous Night Dragon looks shocked, then very angry... then confused.

The dragon has two questions for you, and bellows them so loudly they blow all the torches out. They have to use their fire breath to relight them!

Scribble out every other letter from left to right. Write the letters that are left over on the lines below to reveal the dragon's two questions. The first seven letters have already been done for you.

ĐĐŦƗ€ĐŖ¥ŦØ฿ᵾ⅄SMTLESADLAMQYGRTU

ZBIYLHBOVWSDTIJDQYZOXUPKVNMOFW

GTYHTEJWKAIYMTROIMEYTLNAUIHR

DID YOU S_ _ _ _ _
_ _ _ _ _ _ _ !?

_ _ _ _ _ _ _ _ _ _
_ _ _ _ _ _ _ _ _ _
_ _ _ _ _ _ _ ?!

The dragon has had a jewel stolen too!?
Wait a minute, the second question makes you
think... How did you know the way here?

Who knew how to get into the Clockworkers'
secret spare parts cupboard? Where the Magpies'
secret treasure stash was? And the Squixies'
secret storage den?

Someone has been one step, or one paw, ahead of
you this whole time...

Follow the lines and write the letter from each oval
into the space at the end of each line to reveal a new
word. The first letter of each word has already been
done for you.

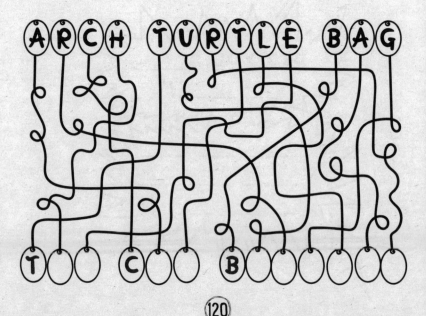

Oh no! As your suspicion grows, you turn back around to ask something but you see that Catsper is already floating away through the tunnels! Quick, catch that cat ghost!

Follow the tangled tunnels. Which one leads you all the way to Catsper?

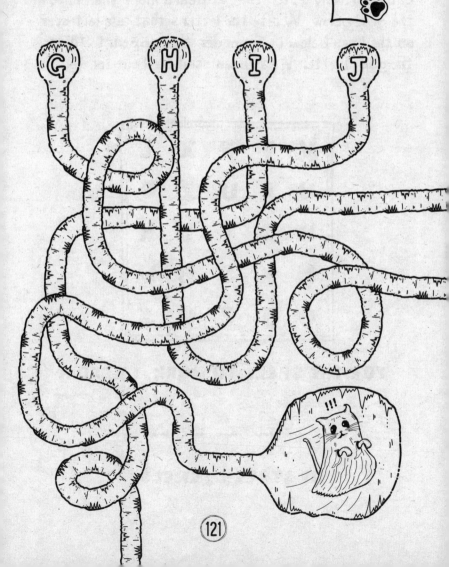

"Okay, okay you got me!" Catsper cries when you catch up, and then confesses everything...

"The truth is, I took the jewels. But I was only borrowing them for a magic spell – then I was going to return them, I promise!"

Cross out any letter that appears more than once in the grid below. Write the letters that are left over on the lines below in the order they appear to fill in the gap. Letter V has been scribbled out for you.

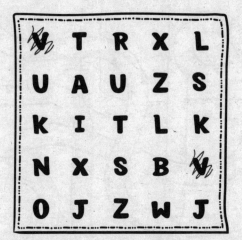

"FOR THE SPELL TO WORK, I NEED A

___ ___ ___ ___ ___ ___ ___

OF STOLEN JEWELS."

Catsper left the trail of clues to make everyone suspicious of each other, thinking you wouldn't be brave enough to follow the clues to the Night Dragon's lair and so the mystery would remain unsolved!

Use the symbol key to crack the code and fill in the gaps to reveal the name of the magic spell that Catsper has stolen all of these jewels for...

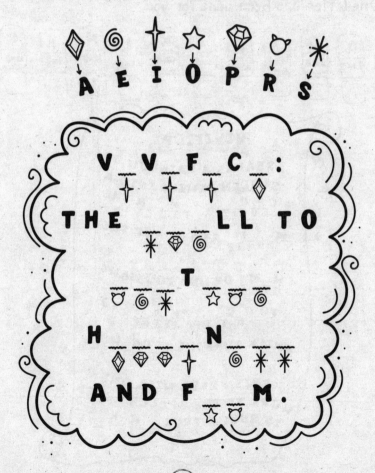

If done correctly, this spell will restore King Cranky's happiness. Then, by giving true happiness to another, Catsper's cat form will be restored so they don't have to live as a ghost any more!

Solve the number problem below each letter in the Key. Then use the answers to fill in the gaps and reveal the step-by-step instructions for the spell. One letter has been done for you.

A	D	E	H	I	K	L	N	R	S
27÷3	2×8	15−9	35÷5	3×7	40÷8	44÷4	11−8	6×3	11−7
						3			

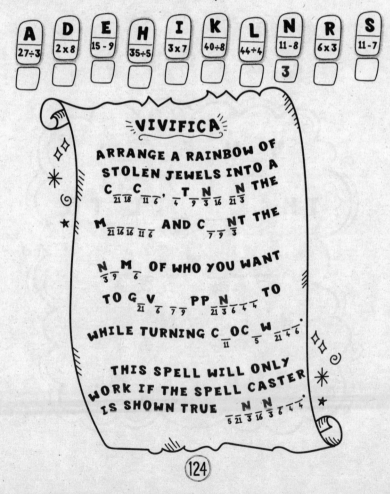

✧ VIVIFICA ✧

ARRANGE A RAINBOW OF STOLEN JEWELS INTO A
C __(21) __(18) C __(11) __(6), T __(4) N __(7) __(9) __(3) __(16) __(21) __(3) THE

M __(21) __(16) __(16) __(11) __(6) AND C __(7) __(9) __(3) NT THE

N __(3) M __(9) __(6) OF WHO YOU WANT

TO G __(21) V __(6) __(7) __(9) PP __(21) N __(3) __(6) __(4) __(4) TO

WHILE TURNING C __(11) OC __(5) W __(21) __(4) __(6)

THIS SPELL WILL ONLY WORK IF THE SPELL CASTER IS SHOWN TRUE __(5) __(21) N __(3) N __(16) __(6) __(4) __(4).

You spend a while thinking about what to do, before deciding to help Catsper arrange the jewels in a circle. Then, you wait to see what happens next...

Can you find all five words from the rainbow of jewels in the wordsearch below? Words may be hidden horizontally or vertically.

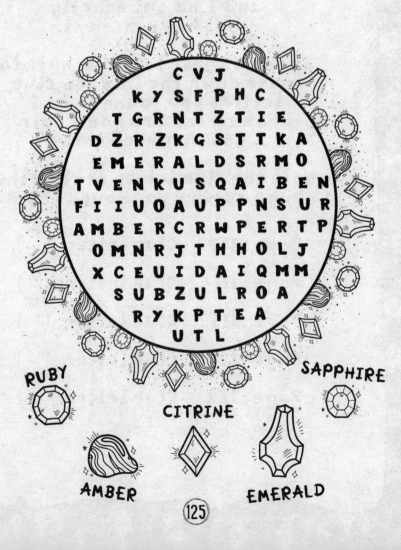

```
        C V J
      K Y S F P H C
    T G R N T Z T I E
  D Z R Z K G S T T K A
  E M E R A L D S R M O
T V E N K U S Q A I B E N
F I I U O A U P P N S U R
A M B E R C R W P E R T P
O M N R J T H H O L J
X C E U I D A I Q M M
  S U B Z U L R O A
    R Y K P T E A
      U T L
```

RUBY

SAPPHIRE

CITRINE

AMBER

EMERALD

CLUE LOGBOOK:
Dragon's Lair

In a moment, you will continue
and find out exactly
what happens next.

But first, just take a minute to
write down the last few clue
letters you found in and
around the Dragon's Lair
– you will need them!

Note the clue letter next to the
Page number you found it on:

Page : 107   Clue letter: ◯

Page : 111   Clue letter: ◯

Page : 115   Clue letter: ◯

Page : 121   Clue letter: ◯

Page : 122   Clue letter: ◯

★The story continues...★

When you made the choice to help Catsper perform the Vivifica spell instead of reporting their crimes to King Cranky, you showed true kindness to the spell caster...

So, does that mean the Vivifica spell will work? There's only one way to find out!

Crack the code on the next pages to reveal the end of the story.

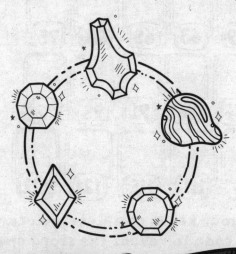

Crack the code to finish the story!

Look back at all five Clue Logbooks on Pages 30, 54, 78, 102 and 126. Write the clue letters into the key below:

(For example, because you found the letter 'M' on Page 13, the letter 'M' is in the '13' box)

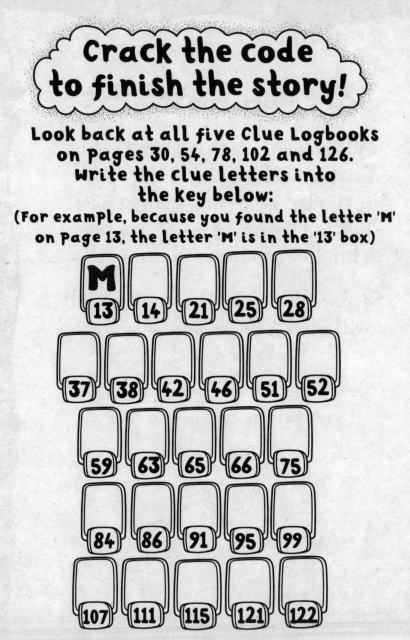

Once your key is complete, you can crack the code to reveal the story ending!

THE SPELL WAS S_____!
42 25 107 107 46 42 42 115 25 63

KING C_____ THE G_____
107 51 111 99 14 84   21 51 25 13 59 84

GOBLIN B_____ KING C_____
28 46 107 86 13 46 42   107 37 46 46 51 84

THE G_____ GOBLIN!
21 63 46 46 115 25 63

H_____ IS R_____
37 111 59 59 75 99 46 42 42   51 46 42 66 86 51 46 95

TO THE WHOLE KINGDOM.

C_____ IS NO L_____ A G_____.
107 111 66 42 59 46 51   63 86 99 21 46 51   21 37 86 42 66

TOGETHER, YOU R_____ ALL THE
51 46 66 25 51 99

S_____ J_____, EXCEPT ONE...
42 66 86 63 46 99   121 46 122 46 63 42

NOW THAT K____ C_____ IS
14 75 99 21   107 37 46 46 51 84

FEELING SO G_____, YOU
21 46 99 46 86 25 42

CAN KEEP THE E_____!
46 13 46 51 111 63 95

Congratulations

You've completed your quest!
The adventure isn't over
just yet...

You'll find more Puzzle Quest fun
online at collins.co.uk/puzzlequest

But wait!

You'll need the secret password...

Use the key from page 128 to crack
the code and reveal your answer!

The secret password is

$\overline{107}$ $\overline{37}$ $\overline{46}$ $\overline{46}$ $\overline{51}$ $\overline{84}$

PUZZLE

Answers

Page 10 – Sequence Puzzle

13   27
6   20   34

8   24
16   32   40

36
31   26   21   16

Page 12 – Silhouette Match

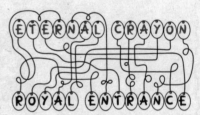

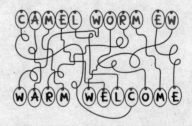

Page 11 – Tangled Paths

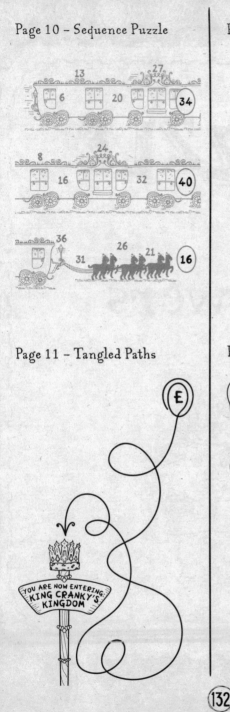

YOU ARE NOW ENTERING
KING CRANKY'S
KINGDOM

Page 13 – Unscramble

ETERNAL CRAYON

ROYAL ENTRANCE

CAMEL WORM EW

WARM WELCOME

Pages 14 & 15 – Kriss Kross

Page 17 – Sudoku

3	4	1	2
1	2	3	4
2	1	4	3
4	3	2	1

1	3	4	2
4	2	3	1
2	4	1	3
3	1	2	4

4	3	1	2
2	1	3	4
3	4	2	1
1	2	4	3

Page 16 – Word Scribble

PICKLED
ONIONS

Page 18 – Code-Cracker

"WELCOME TO
KING CRANKY'S
CASTLE! I'LL BE
YOUR GUIDE.
FOLLOW ME
CLOSELY BECAUSE
THE ENCHANTED
CASTLE PATHS
MOVE AROUND
A LOT!"

Page 19 – Follow the Path

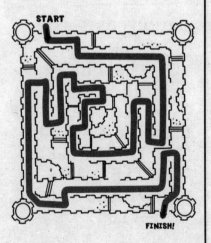

Page 20 – Maze

Page 21 – Word-Wheels

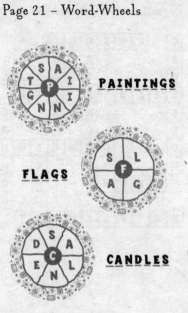

PAINTINGS

FLAGS

CANDLES

Page 22 – Order Game

Page 23 – Odd One Out

Page 24 – Spot the Difference

Page 25 – Wordfinder

LET'S GO TO THE VAULT!

Pages 26 & 27 – Wordsearch

```
        I U X
      V L S R R
     (C O I N S) A J
      B F S T S O C P S
    L T E V I (C R O W N) A
    F (S I L V E R) U P O V   R C
  B O E F T L L U A P K A M   U S
  T B N H T A H J W W P V K O R P S
C C M Y H E R M V S C L M G U D A G H
A U E H I (B R O N Z E) R O   R S T
  T F G Q I S Q H  G  N H L   O R E
  K X A A B Z R O  O  T T D   R T
  (C H A I N S) B  L  N Y C L
    L S Z S A L  E  S P S M
      G E G Y E  S  S E
        O V U T  S  L
        S U S
```

(135)

Page 28 - Maths Game

A $26 + 28 = 54$

B $91 - 33 = 58$

C $6 \times 9 = 54$

D $87 - 33 = 54$

B is the odd one out

Pages 34 & 35 - Wordsearch

Page 29 - Code-Cracker

THAT COG BELONGS
TO ONE OF THE
CLOCKWORKERS!
LET'S GO AND
VISIT THE
CLOCKWORKER
WING OF THE
CASTLE AND SEE
WHAT THEY HAVE
TO DO WITH
ALL THIS...

Page 36 - Spot the Difference

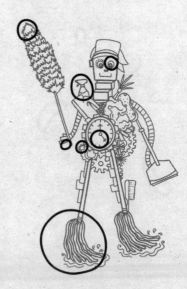

Page 37 – Word-Wheels

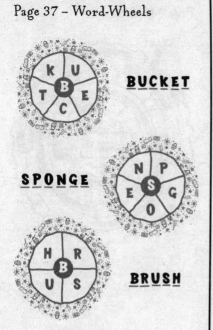

BUCKET

SPONGE

BRUSH

Page 38 – Word Scribble

THE EXPLORATION ROOM

Page 39 – Order Game

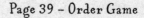
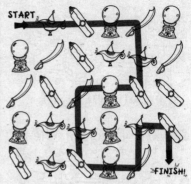

START

FINISH!

Pages 40 & 41 – Kriss Kross

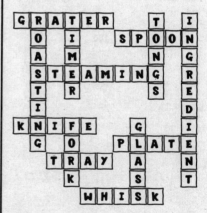

Page 42 – Unscramble

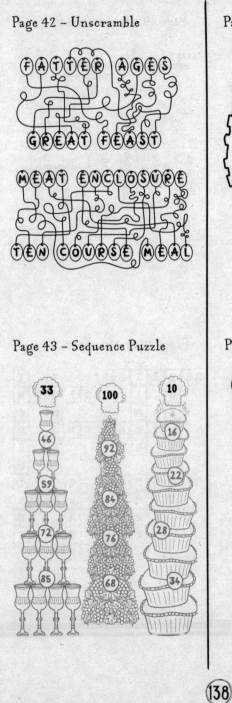

FATTER AGES

GREAT FEAST

MEAT ENCLOSURE

TEN COURSE MEAL

Page 44 – Maze

START

FINISH!

Page 43 – Sequence Puzzle

33

46

59

72

85

100

92

84

76

68

10

16

22

28

34

Page 45 – Silhouette Match

E

THE GREAT BIG GREEDY GOBLIN

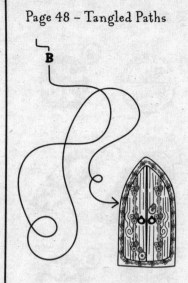

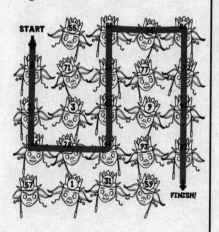

3	2	1	4
4	1	2	3
1	3	4	2
2	4	3	1

2	1	3	4
4	3	2	1
3	4	1	2
1	2	4	3

2	4	1	3
1	3	2	4
3	2	4	1
4	1	3	2

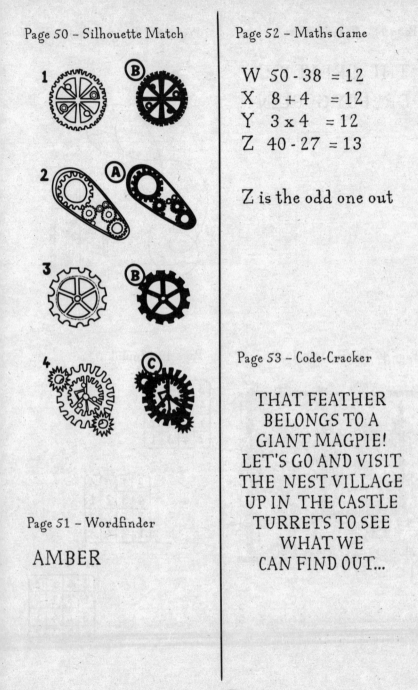

Page 50 – Silhouette Match

1 → B

2 → A

3 → B

4 → C

Page 51 – Wordfinder

AMBER

Page 52 – Maths Game

W 50 - 38 = 12
X 8 + 4   = 12
Y 3 x 4   = 12
Z 40 - 27 = 13

Z is the odd one out

Page 53 – Code-Cracker

THAT FEATHER
BELONGS TO A
GIANT MAGPIE!
LET'S GO AND VISIT
THE NEST VILLAGE
UP IN THE CASTLE
TURRETS TO SEE
WHAT WE
CAN FIND OUT...

Page 58 – Sudoku

4	2	3	1
1	3	4	2
2	4	1	3
3	1	2	4

2	1	3	4
3	4	2	1
4	3	1	2
1	2	4	3

4	3	1	2
2	1	3	4
1	2	4	3
3	4	2	1

Page 60 – Spot the Difference

Page 59 – Word-Wheels

LADDER

STAIRS

ROPES

Page 61 – Wordfinder

141

Pages 62 & 63 – Kriss Kross

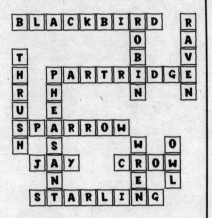

```
B L A C K B I R D    R
            O         A
T     P A R T R I D G E
H     H         B     N
R     E               
U     S P A R R O W    
S     A           O   O
H   J A Y     C R O W  
      N       E       L
    S T A R L I N G
```

Page 64 – Code-Cracker

A – 2	O – 8
C – 4	R – 5
E – 12	S – 7
H – 6	T – 16
L – 13	U – 9
M – 15	W – 14
N – 3	Y – 11

Page 65 – Tangled Paths

Page 66 – Word Scribble

THE ORACLE OWL'S NEST-BUILDING MASTERCLASS

Page 67 – Order Game

START

FINISH!

Page 69 – Unscramble

SHINE SONG WRITING

SINGING IN THE SHOWER

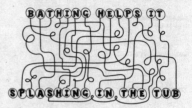

BATHING HELPS IT

SPLASHING IN THE TUB

Page 68 – Sudoku

6   24   99

11   31   84

16   38   69

21   45   54

26   52   39

Page 70 – Maze

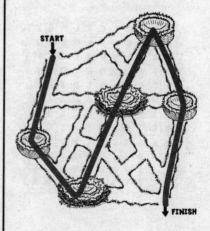

START

FINISH

Page 71 – Maths Game

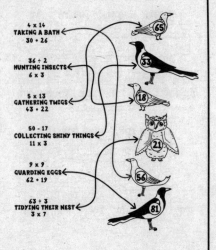

4 x 14
TAKING A BATH ←
30 + 26

36 ÷ 2
HUNTING INSECTS ←
6 x 3

5 x 13
GATHERING TWIGS ←
43 + 22

50 - 17
COLLECTING SHINY THINGS ←
11 x 3

9 x 9
GUARDING EGGS ←
62 + 19

63 ÷ 3
TIDYING THEIR NEST ←
3 x 7

Page 74 – Odd One Out

Pages 72 & 73 – Wordsearch

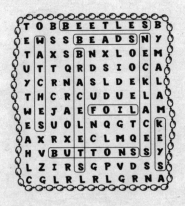

Page 75 – Code-Cracker

SAPPHIRE

Page 76 – Odd One Out

A 9 x 2   = 18
B 54 - 36 = 18
C 72 ÷ 4   = 18
D 9 + 8   = 17

D is the odd one out

Page 82 – Maze

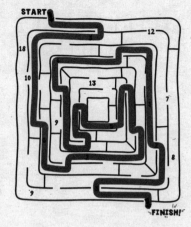

Page 77 – Code-Cracker

THAT ACORN MUST
SURELY BELONG
TO A SQUIXIE!
LET'S GO AND
VISIT THE
GAMING TOWER
AND THE FOREST
TO SEE WHAT
THEY HAVE BEEN
GETTING UP TO...

Page 83 – Follow the Path

Page 84 – Code-Cracker

FLUFFY, SQUEAKY AND CHEEKY

Page 86 – Word Scribble

CHASE THE ACORN

Page 85 – Silhouette Match

Page 87 – Order Game

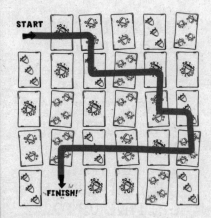

Page 88 – Sequence Puzzle

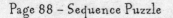

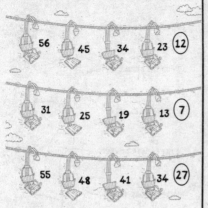

56 45 34 23 (12)

31 25 19 13 (7)

55 48 41 34 (27)

Pages 90 & 91 – Kriss Kross

Page 89 – Unscramble

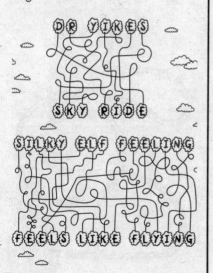

DR YIKES → SKY RIDE

SILKY ELF FEELING → FEELS LIKE FLYING

Pages 92 & 93 – Wordsearch

HIDE

Page 94 – Odd One Out

E

Page 96 – Maths Game

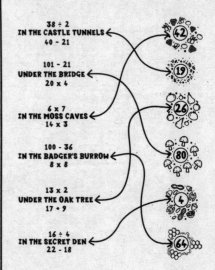

38 ÷ 2
IN THE CASTLE TUNNELS ←
40 – 21

101 – 21
UNDER THE BRIDGE ←
20 x 4

6 x 7
IN THE MOSS CAVES ←
14 x 3

100 – 36
IN THE BADGER'S BURROW ←
8 x 8

13 x 2
UNDER THE OAK TREE ←
17 ÷ 9

16 ÷ 4
IN THE SECRET DEN ←
22 – 18

Page 95 – Anagrams

SERERIB → BERRIES

SOMMRUSHO → MUSHROOMS

STUN → NUTS

TRUFI → FRUIT

DESSE → SEEDS

Page 97 – Tangled Paths

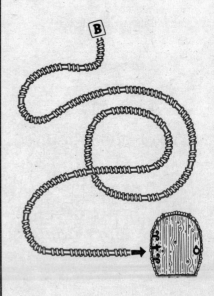

B

Page 98 – Sudoku

1	4	3	2
2	3	1	4
4	1	2	3
3	2	4	1

2	4	1	3
3	1	2	4
1	3	4	2
4	2	3	1

2	3	4	1
4	1	3	2
3	2	1	4
1	4	2	3

Page 99 – Word-Wheels

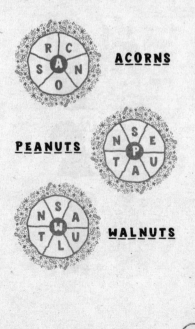

ACORNS

PEANUTS

WALNUTS

Page 100 – Wordfinder

SCALES

Page 101 – Code-Cracker

THESE SCALES
MUST SURELY
BELONG TO A
NIGHT DRAGON!
SHOULD WE EVEN
DARE TO GO
DOWN UNDER
THE CASTLE
DUNGEONS TO
SEE WHAT
WE CAN FIND...?

Page 106 – Maze

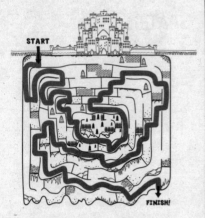

START

FINISH!

Page 108 – Order Game

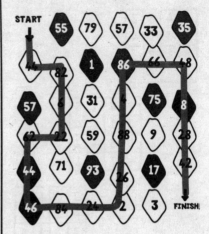

START

FINISH!

Page 107 – Word-Wheels

LAMPS

LANTERNS

TORCHES

Page 109 – Silhouette Match

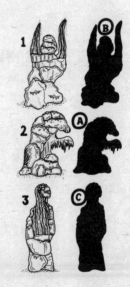

1   B

2   A

3   C

Page 110 – Sequence Puzzle

Page 112 – Odd One Out

Page 111 – Maths Game

A $59 + 33 = 92$

B $123 - 33 = 90$

C $180 \div 2 = 90$

D $9 \times 10 = 90$

A is the odd one out

Page 113 – Order Game

Page 114 – Suduko

3	1	2	4
4	2	3	1
2	4	1	3
1	3	4	2

4	1	2	3
3	2	4	1
1	4	3	2
2	3	1	4

1	3	4	2
4	2	1	3
2	4	3	1
3	1	2	4

Page 115 – Code-Cracker

LOUD, HEAVY FOOTSTEPS

Pages 116 & 117 – Kriss Kross

Page 118 – Spot the Difference

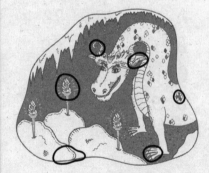

Page 119 – Word Scribble

DID YOU STEAL
MY RUBY!?

HOW DID YOU
KNOW THE WAY
TO MY LAIR?!

Page 121 – Tangled Paths

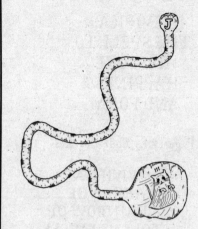

Page 120 – Unscramble

Page 122 – Wordfinder

"FOR THE SPELL
TO WORK,
I NEED A
RAINBOW
OF STOLEN
JEWELS."

Page 123 – Code-Cracker

VIVIFICA:
THE SPELL TO
RESTORE
HAPPINESS
AND FORM.

Page 124 – Code-Cracker

VIVIFICA
ARRANGE
A RAINBOW OF
STOLEN JEWELS
INTO A CIRCLE,
STAND IN THE
MIDDLE AND
CHANT THE
NAME OF WHO
YOU WANT TO
GIVE HAPPINESS
TO WHILE
TURNING
CLOCKWISE.

THIS SPELL WILL
ONLY WORK IF THE
SPELL CASTER
IS SHOWN
TRUE KINDNESS.

A – 9   K – 5
D – 16   L – 11
E – 6   N – 3
H – 7   R – 18
I – 21   S – 4

Page 125 – Wordsearch

Page 128 – Clue Code

THE SPELL WAS
SUCCESSFUL!
KING CRANKY THE
GRUMPY GOBLIN
BECOMES KING
CHEERY THE
GLEEFUL GOBLIN!
HAPPINESS IS
RESTORED TO THE
WHOLE KINGDOM.

CATSPER IS NO
LONGER A GHOST.
TOGETHER, YOU
RETURN ALL THE
STOLEN JEWELS,
EXCEPT ONE...

NOW THAT KING
CHEERY IS
FEELING SO
GENEROUS, YOU
CAN KEEP THE
EMERALD!

NOTES

(Blank 'notes' pages like this are handy for jotting down any notes or working out when you're busy solving puzzles!

You could also use them to write, doodle or anything else you'd like to do while on your quest!)

★ NOTES ★

★ NOTES ★